The Adventures of Scuba Jack
Copyright 2021 by Beth Costanzo
All rights reserved

While there are *plenty* of animals in the animal kingdom, some animals are instantly recognizable. When I say the words giraffe, zebra, or lion, you know exactly what I'm talking about. You can envision their appearance, whether it is their skin color, powerful muscles, or even the way they sound.

www.adventuresofscubajack.com

Today, I want to talk about one of these instantly recognizable animals. That animal is **the tiger**. Even if you haven't seen a tiger in person, you know that a tiger has those famous black stripes on an orange body. But beyond its appearance, there are plenty of fascinating facts about the tiger. At the end of this article, you will be in even more awe with these unbelievable creatures.

www.adventuresofscubajack.com

Let's start this exploration of tigers by returning to their appearance. While the orange tiger is most frequently known, there are actually *three* other color variants for tigers. This means that there are white tigers, golden tigers, and stripeless snow-white tigers. These types of tigers are much more difficult to see in the wild, however. This is because of reduced tiger populations in the wild. You'll most likely see an orange tiger if you visit your local zoo or see a tiger in the wild.

www.adventuresofscubajack.com

In terms of height and weight, male tigers are almost always bigger and heavier than female tigers. Male tigers are about 8 to 13 feet and weigh between 200 and 700 pounds. Females, on the other hand, are about 7 to 9 feet and weigh between 140 to 370 pounds. Male and female tigers also have long tails. Those tails measure between 2 and 3.5 feet.

www.adventuresofscubajack.com

Like other animals, tigers need to eat. Like other big cats, tigers like to hunt large and medium-sized mammals. Some animals on tigers' menu include deer, wild boar, monkeys, and ground-based birds. They have also been seen eating animals like pythons, leopards, and even bears. Tigers like to hunt at night. Compared to animals that hunt in groups (like lions), tigers hunt alone. When they are hunting, tigers aggressively attack their prey, mostly targeting their throats! They wrestle their prey to the ground, continuing to keep their mouths on prey's mouth until it passes away.

Along with hunting by themselves, tigers need their alone time. They block off certain land or territory where they often roam. Unlike other big cats (like leopards), tigers do not climb trees. Instead, tigers are known to be *strong swimmers*. They aren't afraid to get into water and cool off when the weather gets warm.

www.adventuresofscubajack.com

Tigers don't have many natural predators. However, one of their biggest threats is humans. *Habitat destruction* caused by humans has led to many tigers disappearing from our planet. *Poaching* is another bad activity from humans that has led to fewer tigers roaming the Earth. There is good news, however. There are groups of humans who are working hard to protect tigers' health and wildlife. For example, environmental groups have created Tiger Conversation Units, which are blocks of land where tigers can safely roam and live. It's a good start, but it is going to take a lot more work from humans to increase the population of tigers in the wild.

www.adventuresofscubajack.com

BABY TIGERS

In this discussion of tigers, we haven't yet talked about one important thing. **Baby tigers** are some of the most adorable creatures on our planet.

www.adventuresofscubajack.com

When female tigers get pregnant, they are usually pregnant for about *100 days*. They usually give birth to 2 or 3 baby tiger cubs at a time, but some female tigers may give birth to 6 cubs at once. The cubs are born with their eyes closed and they weigh about two to four pounds. In fact, tiger cubs' eyes are closed for about 6 to 14 days before they open them.

At about 2 weeks old, tiger cubs develop *milk teeth*, which they can then use to feed from their mothers. When they are about *8 weeks* old, tiger cubs transition from *milk* to *meat*. When tiger cubs are about 11 months old, they can go hunting by themselves. They separate from their mothers when they're about 2 years old, but these tiger cubs actually continue growing until they're about 5.

www.adventuresofscubajack.com

As you can see, tiger cubs mature very quickly. However, tiger cubs' years are very dangerous. According to one study, about half of tiger cubs don't make it to their second birthday. Those that do, however, can live independent and healthy lives.

www.adventuresofscubajack.com

MORE FUN FACTS

Tigers are some of our planet's most fascinating creatures. They are beautiful, cunning, and deadly. That said, we have only scratched the surface about tigers. Here are some more *fun facts* about this awe-inspiring animal.

www.adventuresofscubajack.com

- In Ancient Rome, humans kept tigers in captivity. These tigers were paraded around Ancient Rome and would even fight against humans in the Colosseum!

- While tigers mate throughout the year, most tiger cubs are born between March and June.

- Sometimes, male tigers take a more active role in raising their cubs. Having said this, it is more often the mother's responsibility.

- Tigers live for about 25 years.

- Tigers' padded feet make it easier for them to stay quiet when walking. This helps them when they are hunting prey.

www.adventuresofscubajack.com

- While tigers' stripes look very similar, there are no two tigers that have the same exact stripes.

- Tigers are known for their roar. Their roar can be so powerful that it can be heard 2 miles away.

- Tigers have white spots on the back of the ears. It is thought that these spots can prevent potential predators from attacking tigers from the rear.

TIGERS ACTIVITIES

TRACING

Trace the sentence then rewrite it

Tiger starts with T

www.adventuresofscubajack.com

COUNTING

Count the tiger cubs and circle the correct answers

8 7 6	5 7 6
7 9 8	7 6 8

www.adventuresofscubajack.com

MAZE

Help the little cub to find his family

www.adventuresofscubajack.com

WORD SEARCH

Find the words listed below

```
T H D M T X S N
S Y U C C L V E
E S A N A U P J
R T R M T I B W
O V I E R I H S
F N T T G I N M
A D S P T I P G
R L M E P N T N
```

- Tigers
- Cubs
- Forest
- White
- Stripe
- Animals
- Hunting
- Cat

www.adventuresofscubajack.com

DOT TO DOT

Follow the dots then color the tiger

www.adventuresofscubajack.com

JIGSAW PUZZLE

Cut out all the pieces of the puzzle and then fit them together to form a picture!

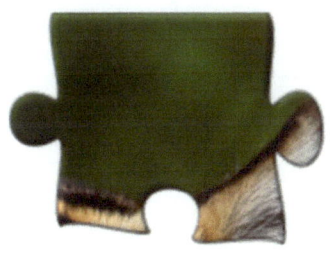

TIGER CUB CRAFT

CRAFT

You will need:

Scissors
Glue
Coloring Pencils

Directions:

1- Glue the front body on the back body
2- Glue the head to the front body
3- Glue the tail behind the back body
4- Glue the front legs to the front body
4- Color your cute Tiger Cub!

www.adventuresofscubajack.com

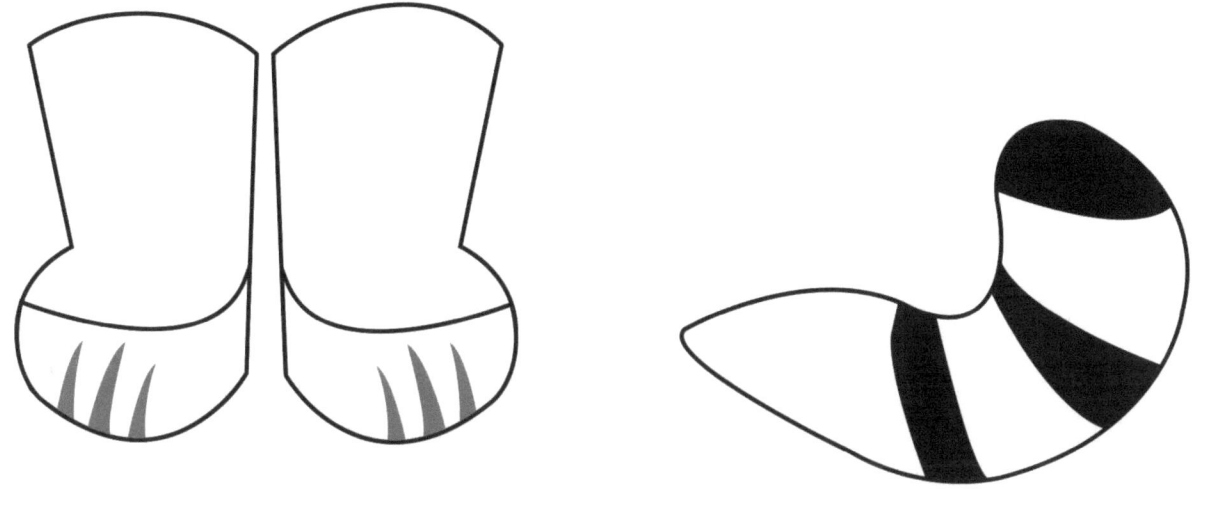

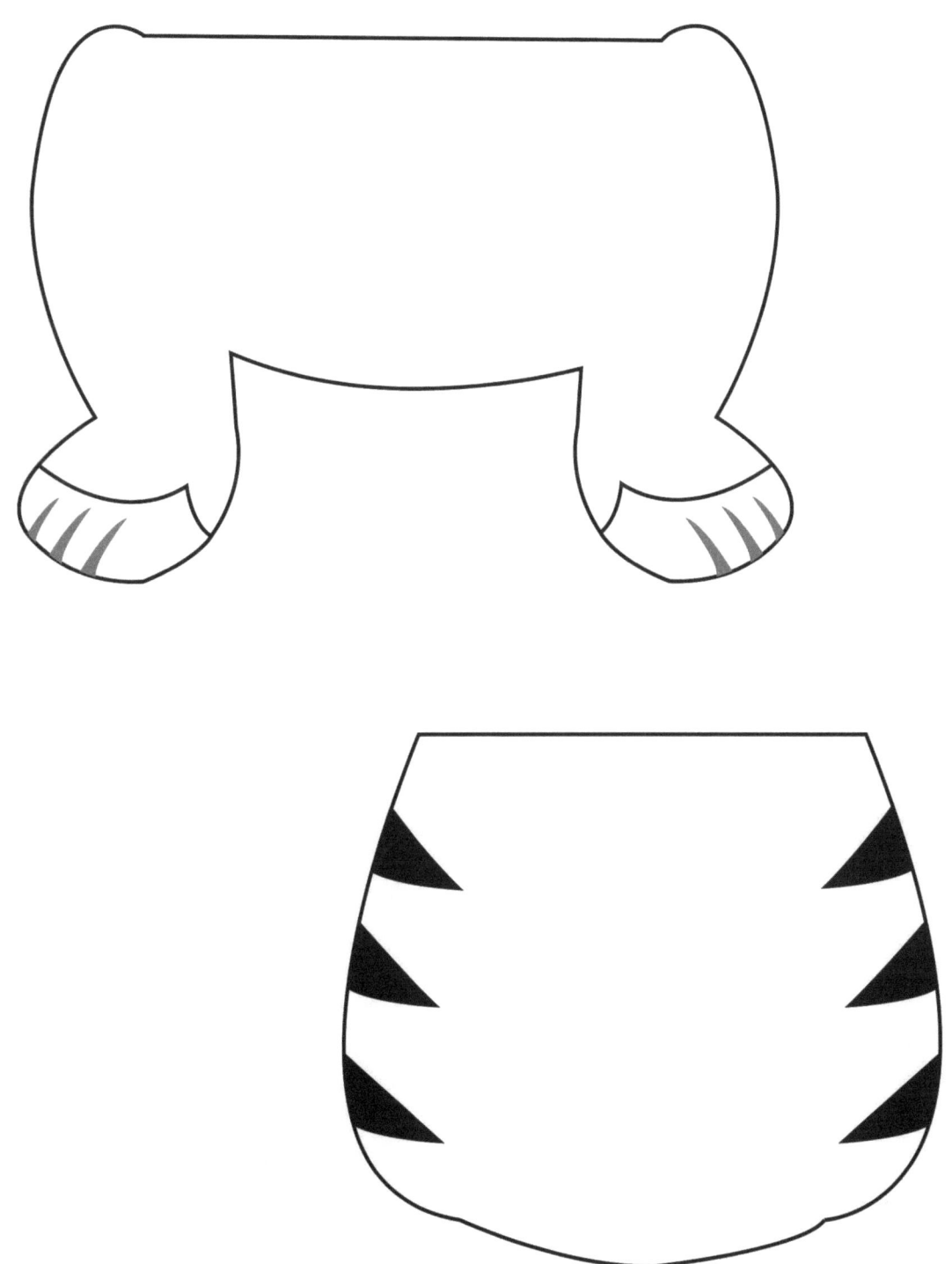

Visit us at:
www.adventuresofscubajack.com

www.ingramcontent.com/pod-product-compliance
Lightning Source LLC
Chambersburg PA
CBHW041435010526
44118CB00002B/78